THE WONDERFUL WORLD OF WORDS

16

Ari and His Articles

Dr Lubna Alsagoff
PhD (Stanford)

 **Marshall Cavendish** Children

Ari was the king's page.
He went everywhere with King Noun.

Ari was in charge of articles.

When **nouns** name things, people, places, ideas and events, they need articles to help them.

THE WONDERFUL WORLD OF WORDS

16

Ari and His Articles

Dr Lubna Alsagoff
PhD (Stanford)

Learn English in a fun and meaningful way!

In this volume, children will learn about articles and how to use them correctly.

Marshall Cavendish

Other Titles in the
Wonderful World of Words (WOW) Series

The castle looks so grand!

I want to live in **a** castle just like the king!

Thank you for lending me **the** umbrella.

Maddy uses **an** umbrella when it is hot and sunny.

Sometimes, even the admiral added some **adjectives** to go along with the **nouns**. Ari had to make sure that there were **articles**.

The admiral needs to buy **an** extra **button** and a **longer** belt. King Noun bought **some** beautiful **flowers** for Queen Verb.

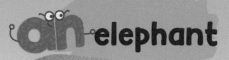

an elephant

an echidna

I like these other animals!

an antelope

an ostrich

5

alligator

bear

cat

dog

iguana

eagle

frog

goat

hyena

Help Ari fill in the blanks.

goat

xerus

raccoon

kiwi

a goes with singular countable nouns that begin with a consonant.

	jaguar		raccoon
	kiwi		seal
	leopard		tiger
	monkey		umbrellabird
	newt		vulture
	ostrich		xerus
	pelican		yak
	quail		zebra

alligator

umbrellabird

an goes with singular countable nouns that begin with a vowel.

But Ari is worried. Just when he thinks he knows what **a** and **an** like, he sees **a** running away and **an** standing in its place!

a frog

an excited frog

a monkey

an upside-down monkey

Then he sees **an** running away and **a** standing in its place!

an iguana

a friendly iguana

an ostrich

a curious ostrich

I wonder what's going on?

Ari made the **articles** stand to attention.

He lined up the words.

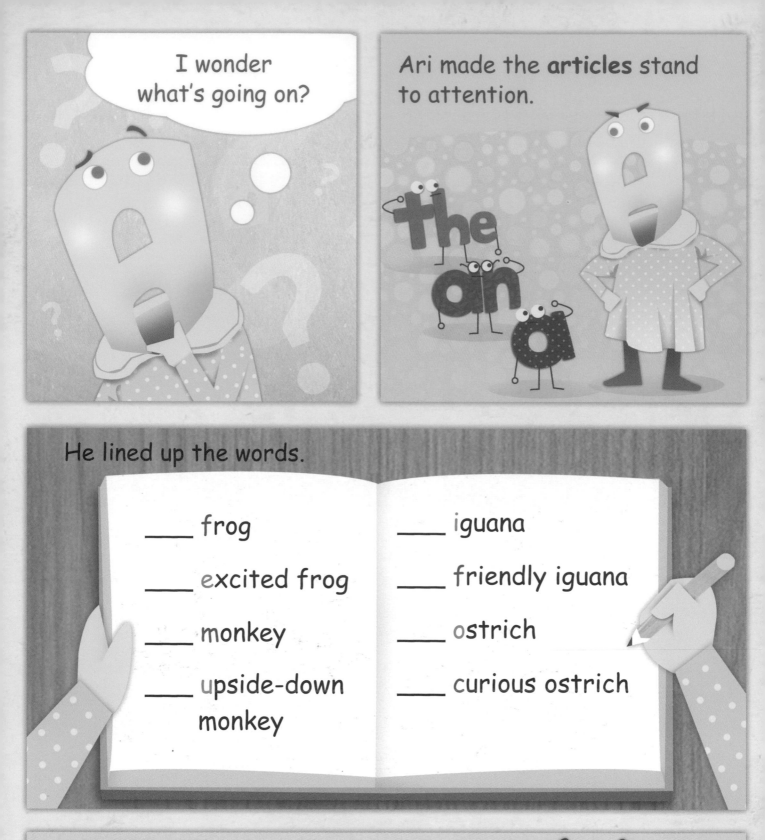

___ frog

___ excited frog

___ monkey

___ upside-down monkey

___ iguana

___ friendly iguana

___ ostrich

___ curious ostrich

Ari saw that *a* could only have consonants following them and *an* could only have vowels following them!

a **f**rog

an **e**xcited frog

a **m**onkey

an **u**pside-down monkey

an **i**guana

a **f**riendly iguana

an **o**strich

a **c**urious ostrich

Ari changed the rules he had written for **a** and **an** to make them better.

a goes before words that begin with consonants.

an goes before words that begin with vowels.

a bird

an angry bird

a very angry bird

an elephant

a polka-dotted elephant

an orange polka-dotted elephant

an orchid

a special orchid

an unusual and special orchid

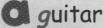

a guitar

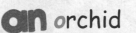

an electric guitar

a wonderful electric guitar

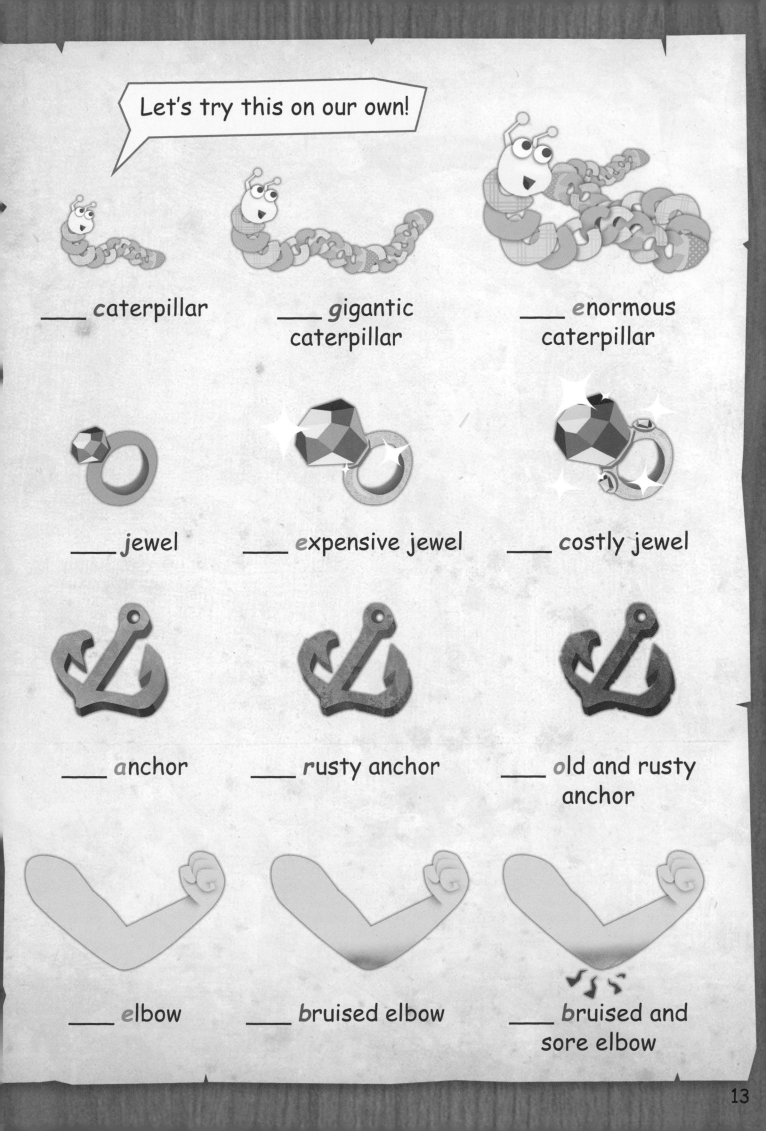

___ caterpillar

___ gigantic
caterpillar

___ enormous
caterpillar

___ jewel

___ expensive jewel

___ costly jewel

___ anchor

___ rusty anchor

___ old and rusty
anchor

___ elbow

___ bruised elbow

___ bruised and
sore elbow

13

Draw red lines to get **a** to nouns that begin with consonants, and blue lines to get **an** to nouns that begin with vowels.

iron

watch

ant

question

idea

answer

rocket

key

eye

escape

rainbow

cup

spider

fork

balloon

14

Let's help Telly the tortoise find her way home. She only likes to eat fruits and vegetables that begin with consonants.

In the Forest of WOW, Owl was teaching a class on articles.

> Articles are very important to nouns.

Rule: Singular nouns need to have a or an.
Plural nouns can be used by themselves!

✓ I need [a pencil]   ✗ I need [pencil]
✓ I need [an eraser]   ✗ I need [eraser]

✓ I need [pencils]
✓ I need [erasers]

a goes with consonants and **an** goes with vowels. This rule is the same for nouns and adjectives that follow the article.

I ate a pear and an apple.

He met an otter
and a chimpanzee.

I ate an enormous pear
and a tiny apple.

He met a busy otter
and an eager chimpanzee.

Then why does it sound funny to say **a** *hour*?

Boar is right. **h** is a consonant, so why does **a** *hour* sound so strange?

There are many words in English where the spelling and the sound don't match.

We spell *hour* with an **h**, but we don't pronounce the **h**. It is a silent **h**.

So the word *hour* sounds exactly like the word *our*.

Yes, both *our* and *hour* begin with a vowel sound.

Owl wrote on the blackboard.

When *h* is silent, then *an* is used.

✓ an hour	✗ a hour
✓ an heir to the throne	✗ a heir to the throne
✓ an honest mistake	✗ a honest mistake

When *u*, *eu* or *ew* make the same sound as the consonant *y* in *you*, then *a* is used.

✓ a niversity	✗ an niversity
✓ a niform	✗ an niform
✓ a seful idea	✗ an seful idea
✓ a e	✗ an e

When *o* makes the same sound as the consonant *w* in *won*, then *a* is used.

✓ a ne-way street	✗ an ne-way street
✓ a ne-kilometre race	✗ an ne-kilometre race

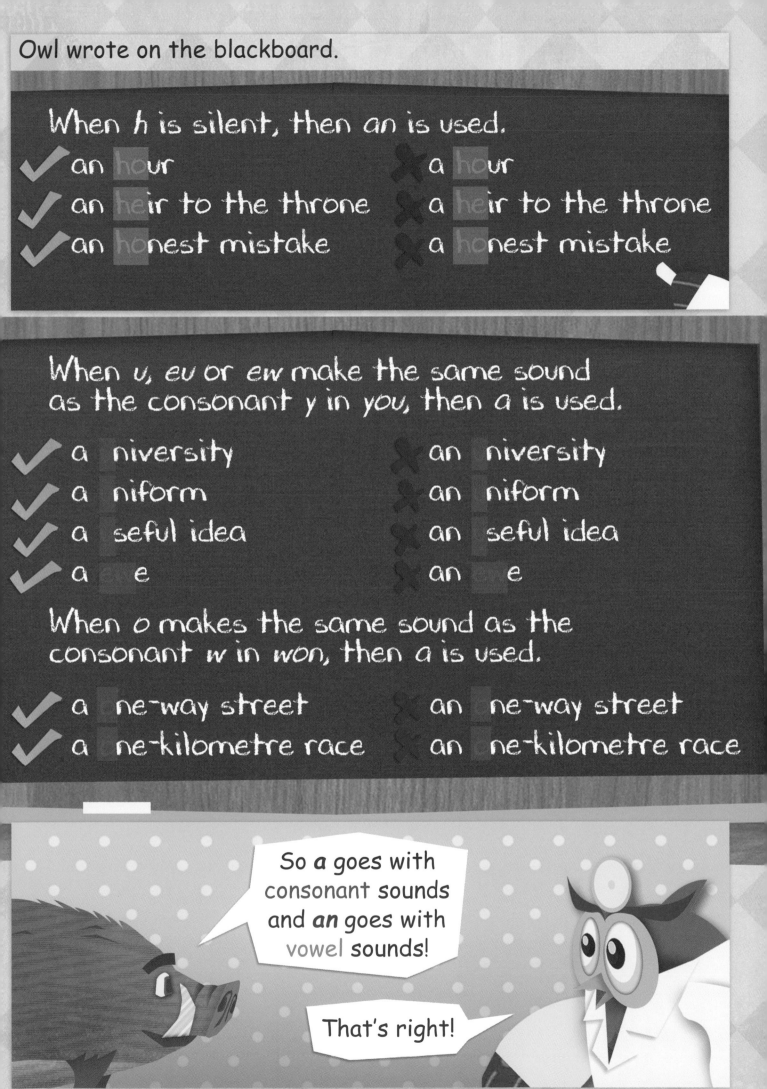

So **a** goes with consonant **sounds** and **an** goes with vowel **sounds**!

That's right!

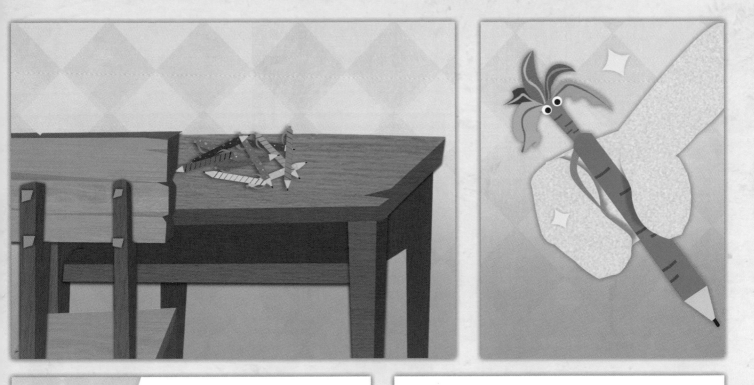

This is **the** pen that I wanted! Thank you!

Why didn't you say you wanted **the** pen with **the** coconut tree on it?

Donkey, you should use **the** when you want to talk about a specific thing or person.

Let's help all the animals in WOW to learn about articles.

Peter the penguin was upset. He needed to walk to [1]_____ hardware store to buy [2]_____ electric drill. His was broken!

[3]_____ nearest store was over [4]_____ kilometre away. That was very far for [5]_____ penguin to walk!

But he really needed [6]_____ drill to hang his pictures.

It was [7]_____ warm afternoon so he took almost [8]_____ hour to get there.

By [9]_____ time he reached [10]_____ store, he was tired and had [11]_____ blister on his foot and [12]_____ terrible headache.

CERTIFICATE OF ACHIEVEMENT

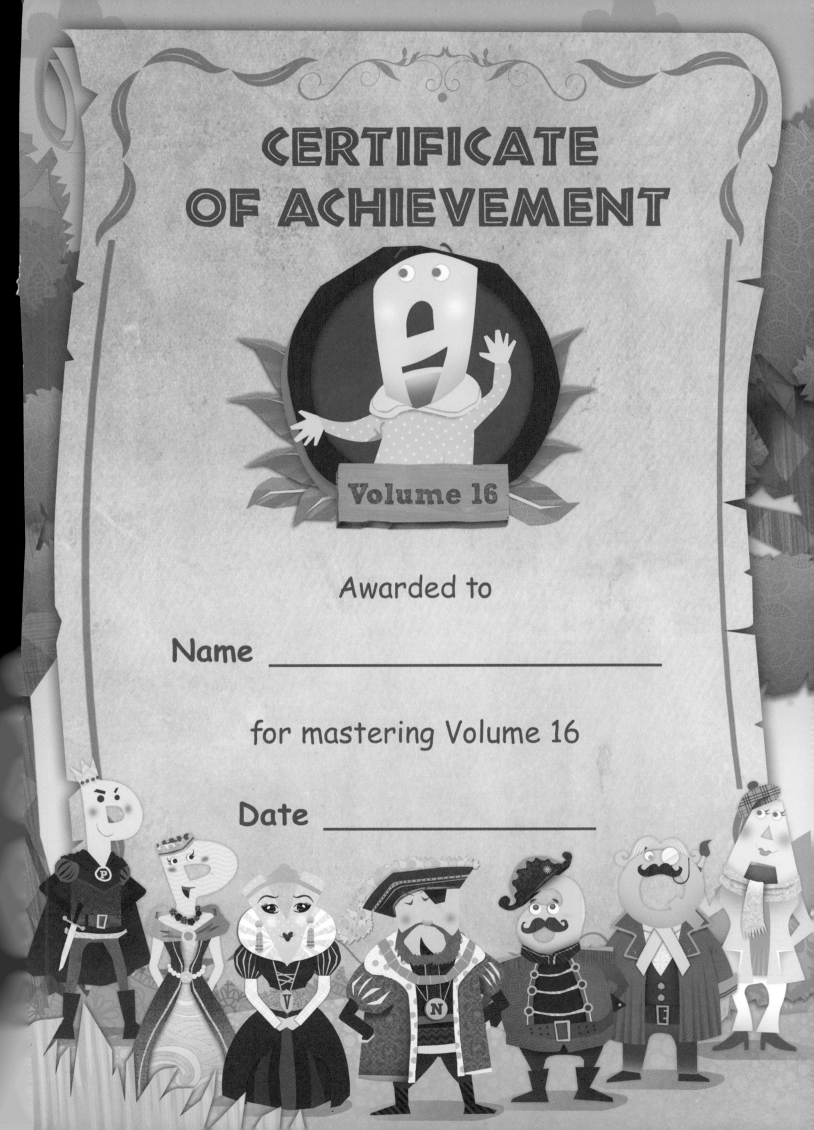

Volume 16

Awarded to

Name _____

for mastering Volume 16

Date _____

Welcome to the **Wonderful World of Words (WOW)**!

This series of books aims to help children learn English grammar in a fun and meaningful way through stories.

Children will read and discover how the people and animals of WOW learn the importance of grammar, as the adventure unfolds from volume to volume.

What's Inside

Imaginative stories that engage children, and help develop an interest in learning grammar

Adventures that encourage children to learn and understand grammar, and not just memorise rules

Games and activities to reinforce learning and check for understanding

About the Author

Dr Lubna Alsagoff is a language educator who is especially known for her work in improving the teaching of grammar in schools and in teacher education. She was Head of English Language and Literature at the National Institute of Education (NIE), and has published a number of grammar resources used by teachers and students. She has a PhD in Linguistics from Stanford University, USA, and has been teaching and researching English grammar for over 30 years.

Published by Marshall Cavendish Children
An imprint of Marshall Cavendish International

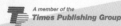
A member of the
Times Publishing Group

Printed in Singapore

visit our website at:
www.marshallcavendish.com

CHILDREN
ISBN 978-981-5009-05-7

9 789815 009057

Seeing his friend, Fran, who wore [13] bright pink uniform with [14] elegant pink boa cheered him up tremendously. Fran was sorry to hear about Peter's headache. So she made him [15] iced tea and shared [16] egg sandwich with him.

She gave him [17] useful brochure to read about [18] different types of drills that [19] store had.

When he decided on [20] drill that he wanted, Fran gave him [21] quick lesson on how to use it.

Fran called for [22] taxi to take Peter home. It was still [23] very warm afternoon.

It wasn't such [24] horrible day after all. He got to see his friend, Fran, and had [25] lovely time with her.

Dear Parents,

In this volume, we learn when to use *a* and *an*.

We learn that *a* is used when the word that follows it begins with a consonant, and *an* is used when the following word begins with a vowel. In school, students are only taught the simple rule that allows them to use *a* and *an* correctly only with a noun, e.g. *an egg*, but they don't learn the rule when there is adjective that comes in between, such as *a boiled egg* and not *an boiled egg*. We also learn that consonants and vowels refer to sounds and not spelling. Hence words with a silent "h" are pronounced with a vowel, so that is why we say *an hour* and not *a hour*.

The is difficult to write rules for. But if you remember that ***the*** is used only when the speaker is referring to a specific thing or person, and it is certain that the hearer also knows about this specific thing or person, ***the*** is used. So when you've mentioned a thing or person, the next time you talk about them, ***the*** is used.

Page	Possible Answers	
13	<u>a</u> caterpillar	<u>an</u> anchor
	<u>a</u> gigantic caterpillar	<u>a</u> rusty anchor
	<u>an</u> enormous caterpillar	<u>an</u> old, rusty anchor
	<u>a</u> jewel	<u>an</u> elbow
	<u>an</u> expensive jewel	<u>a</u> bruised elbow
	<u>a</u> costly jewel	<u>a</u> bruised and sore elbow

14-15

22-23
1. a
2. an
3. the
4. a
5. a
6. a
7. a
8. an
9. the
10. the
11. a
12. a
13. a
14. an
15. an
16. an
17. a
18. the
19. the
20. the
21. a
22. a
23. a
24. a
25. a